OH, I DIDN'T KNOW RETIREMENT IS THIS GREAT!

Gateway to peaceful and prosperous retirement

Copyright©2022 Glory White

All Rights Reserved

TABLE OF CONTENT

Table of Contents

INTRODUCTION

Retirement may be the most enjoyable period of your life. It all depends on how you look at things.

You can perceive things in a new and different light by shifting your perspective. This new perspective can help you shift your mind and come up with new methods to approach a problem, even if it's as simple as figuring out how to retire or feeling anxious about retiring.

Your attitude toward anything in life is determined by your point of view. If you're scared about retiring, it's possible that you just need to shift your mindset.

Many people are concerned about their retirement. Looking at it from a different perspective can modify and improve your feelings about the future, as well as how you prepare for it.

There are so many things to achieve at the retirement period – time to do all you ever desire to do that your work time of 9 to 5 have denied you.

Time to finish that book, time to work as a consultant, time to share life experiences with the younger generation, time to do so much.

The following chapters contain tips on how you can have a change of perspective and also have more than enough money throughout your retirement.

CHAPTER ONE

Here are eight methods to change your mindset about retirement:

1. It's about time, not money

Money is the most valuable currency in our culture. Over 55% of those polled valued money over time, according to the researchers.

Even after controlling for existing levels of available time and money, the researchers discovered that persons who chose time were statistically happier and more satisfied with life than those who chose money.

Another study discovered that persons who were excessively concerned about their retirement funds were happier once they retired, owing to the fact that they had more control over their time. In fact, many people today define retirement as the capacity to manage their own schedule.

If you focus less on money and more on how to spend your time, you could be less concerned about retirement.

2. New Retirement perspective

Retiring in your sixties, on the other hand, is a relatively new concept. For the majority of our history, people worked until they died or were physically unable to work any more. Furthermore, people nowadays live to be well into their 80s and beyond. Never mind that today's 65-year-olds are healthier and stronger than those of just 10 or 20 years ago. Life expectancies are increasing, and seniors are doing more than ever before.

It's possible that 80 will become the new 65! After all, funding retirement would be a lot easier if it didn't have to last so long! Use the NewRetirement Planner, a complete retirement planning tool, to see what happens if you delay or bring ahead your retirement date. A longevity calculator might be useful as well.

3. Retirement is possible at your forties or earlier

Many people are adopting what could be called extreme retirement or Financial Independence, Retire Early on the other side of the 80 is the new 65 perspective. They are in their 30s or 40s when they retire.

These folks make the decision that financial freedom is more important than spending money. They live exceedingly frugally and save as much money as they can while working – frequently two jobs. They continue to monitor their pennies when they retire, but they are no longer working at a young age. Many people continue to work and make money doing things they enjoy, but they are relieved of the stress of needing to work today in order to pay for tomorrow's expenses.

Others enjoy a few years of retirement while they are still young — before they even begin working.

4. Check - Is Your Present Way of Life Appropriate for Retirement?

Most financial counsellors assume that when we retire, we would continue to spend as we have done throughout our lives. While this is true for the majority of us, many retirees are able to drastically lower their spending. When we retire, we won't have to maintain the status quo.

While working and raising children, what you need to spend to be comfortable may be considerably different from what you need to spend when you retire. And, if you plan to retire somewhere less expensive than where you currently reside, the amount you'll need to save could be drastically different.

Are you willing to adjust your mind about how much money you'll need in retirement to be happy? To see what happens to your finances if you cut your spending, use the NewRetirement, Retirement Planner. It's simple to get started, and after you've established the foundations of your retirement plan, you can add specifics, make modifications, and see how they affect your future right away.

5. Retirement is a New Beginning, Not an End

Retirement represents a fresh start, an opportunity to try new things and live the life they desire.

Second occupations are becoming increasingly popular, and retirees are taking up new hobbies, volunteering, and much more.

In reality, retirement may bring you a slew of new starts.

Retirement is a multi-phase process. After we stop working, most of us will go through a number of transitions.

6. Don't Set a Deadline for Retirement — slide into it!

People used to choose a date for their retirement and throw a large party. You went to work for one day and then didn't come back.

A rising number of people nowadays have a different opinion on when they should retire. Working part-time for a few years or finding a retirement job is how today's retirees move into retirement.

7. IDEAL TIME TO SPEND YOUR MONEY

You've worked and saved your entire life, paying off your mortgage and putting money aside for retirement.

Retirement is the ideal time to spend your money. This is a big shift in perspective, and it concerns many people.

Researchers discovered that in 2015, 30% of persons aged 65 and older with at least $100,000 in savings withdrew less than 1% from their accounts, much below the 4 percent withdrawal rate recommended by many financial counsellors.

Many people are concerned that if they spend all of their money, they may run out. If this describes you, one of the following strategies may help:

Invest in a Savings Account:

You can divide your savings into several categories. You may have accounts for the following:

- **Your requirements** – money needed to make ends meet — prudently invested.

- **Wants** — money for enjoyment and leisure — are also less risky investments.

- **Money set aside for future needs**, emergencies, and more, with the goal of long-term growth.

Make a detailed budget for all of your future expenses.

PlannerPlus from NewRetirement allows you to establish a thorough budget for all future spending in 75 different categories, including your own. You can specify how much you need to spend as well as how much you want to spend. You can also use the system to change your expenditure over time, customize tax treatment, and more.

You might develop the confidence you need to spend money by becoming more thorough about your expenditures.

Lifetime Income (Annuities)

According to studies, people are less concerned about their retirement if they receive a sufficient guaranteed lifelong income. With an annuity, you can turn some of your investments into lifetime income.

When you buy an annuity, you're exchanging a lump sum payment for a lifetime of guaranteed income that will last as long as you do, no matter how long that may be.

You can use an annuity calculator to estimate income or the Retirement Planner to evaluate how an annuity would affect your entire retirement finances.

Any of these methods can assist you in spending responsibly. Use the Retirement Planner to test them out.

8. Make a plan!

Sure, we should have all had a precise financial strategy throughout our lives. However, most of us were able to get by on a month-to-month or year-to-year basis, which was OK as long as we were employed and generating money.

In retirement, we must learn to survive for an extended period of time with a large number of unknowns and a limited set of resources. This is why adopting a fresh approach to financial planning is so vital. At this point in your life, you need a specialized and thorough retirement plan.

The NewRetirement Retirement Planner makes planning and managing your financial future simple.

CHAPTER TWO

<u>7 Ways to Conquer Your Fear of Spending Your Retirement Funds</u>

It's not uncommon for people to be concerned about their retirement savings. Indeed, the majority of people are concerned about depleting their savings and running out of cash. After all, you've been conditioned to earn rather than spend for decades.

When you first received your first pay check, you were probably a teenager, and you had officially begun the cycle of earning and spending your own money. The following procedure has never halted since then:

Work - Earn money - Spend - Save - Work - Earn money - Spend - Save and the circle continues.

And now, just as you're getting ready to retire, you're being forced to transition to a completely new system. It's suddenly meant to seem quite normal to spend - then go ahead and spend some more - then go out and spend even more, depleting the retirement fund you worked so hard to build?

That can be quite frightening! And, if you're terrified, know that you're not alone.

How to Get Over Your Fear of Spending Your Retirement Funds

Here are a few pointers to help you overcome your phobia of spending in retirement.

1) Use a comprehensive retirement expenditure calculator to familiarize yourself with your numbers

It's nearly hard to look at your savings and know that you'll be able to live comfortably in retirement. Simply put, there are too many variables to consider.

Someone else can easily tell you that you have enough money for retirement. However, seeing it for oneself is far more powerful. It's simple to figure out how a full set of your own values — assets, spending, rates of return, inflation, income, and so on — will lead to a secure future. You'll be able to obtain a sense of financial well-being and confidence, as well as overcoming retirement worries, with this extensive knowledge and advanced calculations.

As a result, NewRetirement has developed the most comprehensive retirement planning solution available. The greatest retirement spending calculator with full budgeting and withdrawal possibilities is included into the functionality.

Begin by entering some basic information to determine how long your funds will last. Then, by adding more detail and running numerous scenarios, you'll be able to determine your own safe spending limits. The withdrawals tool will assist you in determining how to best manage your savings withdrawals. And, for the rest of your life, you can readily view your predicted annual income and expenses.

Continue to add details, reconcile your data, and stay on pace for a secure future.

2) Recognize the Real Threats to Your Security in the Future (and plan wisely)

According to studies, the three largest retirement fears are running out of money, doubts about the viability of Social Security, and not being able to afford healthcare.

Inflation, unstable economic markets, unforeseen emergencies, forced retirement, plummeting property values, an environmental disaster, a catastrophic health incident, or even an unpredictable pandemic are all potential threats to your financial stability.

There is a lot we can't foresee about the future, but that doesn't mean you can't plan! You'll feel a lot better about retiring after using NewRetirement Planner to discover how to plan for the unknown.

3) Consult with a financial advisor.

Speaking with a financial counselor might put your mind at ease about whether your savings will last as long as you want them to.

A financial advisor can also assist you with:

- Retirement fund management

- Mortgage guidance

- Insurance tips to help you get the most out

of your money.

- Tax assistance

- Investing risk

- Estate planning

4) Invest in a Lifetime Annuity to Secure Your Income

A lifelong annuity is a type of insurance that allows you to pay a single sum and get a guaranteed monthly payment for the rest of your life (no matter how long that turns out to be).

In other words, if you have $275,000 and want to receive a fixed payment each month rather than worrying about what investments to make that won't go bankrupt and would yield your desired income, you might buy an instant annuity and receive $1,100 every month. (This is only an example; the actual amount varies for everyone.) Calculate your income with a lifelong annuity calculator.

The constant pay may be just what you need to put your retirement worries to rest. When looking at your funds as a whole, it was difficult to predict how long they would last, but now that you have $1,100 coming in from social security, you can see how this is working.

The disadvantage of lifetime annuities is that they are not intended to provide you with high rates of return on your investment. They're intended to take away your worries about retirement and provide you some peace of mind.

Advantages of Annuities

Annuities have a number of advantages over other types of retirement investments, particularly for people who cannot or do not want to risk losing a percentage of their retirement assets due to stock or bond market fluctuations.

Annuities offer the following benefits:

● **Lifetime Income** - An immediate lifetime annuity contract ensures that you will receive periodic payments for the rest of your life. The insurance company that provides the annuity bears the risk of you having a long and happy life.

Social Security and pensions provide similar retirement income protection, but only to a limited extent. The only restriction on the size of your periodic annuity payment is the amount of money you have available to buy an annuity now. Even better for many retirees, the higher your monthly payments are for the same amount, the older you are.

• **Protection from Inflation -** With annuities, you can assure that your monthly income keeps up with the cost of living.

Because inflation can have a severe effect on your investments, this is vital. The disadvantage of an add-on like inflation protection is that it will cost you more in the long run, either in terms of initial charges or smaller rewards once you start collecting.

● **Safeguard from Principals** – One of the most appealing characteristics of fixed- and equity-indexed annuities is that the annuity's value can be guaranteed to be equal to or greater than the amount invested. You can rest assured that you (or your heirs) will receive at least the same amount of money as you put into the annuity.

- **Safeguard from Taxes** - Buying an annuity with eligible retirement funds instead of getting a lump sum payment can save you money on taxes.

There are no tax penalties for rolling over qualified funds into a qualified annuity. Only the income generated by the annuity is taxed.

- **Predictability:**

Knowing how much money you'll have in retirement (hopefully enough to cover all of your expenses) can make you feel better. That kind of predictability is available with lifetime annuities.

Retirees who must withdraw money from their savings to cover retirement expenses, on the other hand, face increased financial concern.

In conclusion, an annuity is an excellent strategy to safeguard your retirement quality of life. Your retirement savings can be utilized to buy guaranteed income that will endure for as long as you need it. The best part is that this income is immune to inflation and other financial concerns.

Disadvantages of Annuities

- **Annuities Are Not All Created Equal** - Some annuities, particularly fixed annuities, are seen as a good solution to most retirees' desire for guaranteed income by the financial planning community. Other annuity products, on the other hand, have a bad reputation. Some advisors believe they are an overpriced and useless product. It is critical that you comprehend the many features and phrases associated with annuities.

- **Lower Returns on Investment (ROI)** – You forego the possibility to earn higher returns by investing in assets that fluctuate in value, such as stocks, in exchange for the retirement income certainty given by fixed annuities or equity-indexed annuities. A fixed annuity is a safe and conservative investment, but it does not allow you to view the potential returns (and losses) of a more risky investment.

- **Exorbitant Fees:** Sales commissions and maintenance fees are common annuity complaints. And there are occasions when costs are simply too high. It is essential that you shop around for an annuity and understand exactly what you are paying for.

- **Unpredictable** - Annuities are less predictable than alternative retirement solutions. You don't have access to that lump sum of money after you buy an annuity contract because your capital is locked up in the annuity.

According to several retirement financial advisers, people should set aside at least 40% of their retirement assets for unforeseen emergencies. Because most annuities are designed to offer a consistent stream of income over time, they aren't ideal for covering significant, unexpected bills.

5) Don't Let Your Bank Account Get Too Low

This option is more difficult to implement than it appears, but it is entirely achievable. Many retirees are able to build their wealth rather than deplete it when they retire.

If you've already decided that you'd like to leave a sizable inheritance to your children and grandkids, this option may be ideal for you.

Since the early 1900s, the stock market has returned around 7% each year on average. You've most likely witnessed its expansion and can attest to the growth rate. However, over the last 100 years, there have been many ups and downs, and now that you're approaching retirement, you need more assurance regarding returns than ever before. I'm betting you'll be aiming for 3-5 percent returns on your assets.

The guideline of four percent...

According to many investing pros, taking 4 percent withdrawals from your assets is one strategy to assure that you will have money when you die.

However, this isn't a hard and fast rule. Some feel that 4% is too much, while others argue that it is too little.

What's more, you know what? They're both correct because everyone's circumstances are unique, resulting in a unique scenario, and no one can forecast how the stock market will perform.

If you're worried about running out of money in retirement, simply withdraw a percentage of your savings that is less than or equal to your rate of return.

To put it another way, aim to withdraw your money at a rate of 2% to 3%. It's unlikely to shrink, and you'll always be reassured that you're being extremely frugal with your hard-earned cash.

6) Exchanging Cash for a More Valuable Asset - Time

Money isn't as crucial as time.

A man lies on his deathbed with just a few minutes to live, as the story goes. He's aware of it, and his family is aware of it, but there's nothing anyone can do about it. What is that man's one desire? Time.

He considers the opportunities he's passed up, the memories he's forgotten, and the time he's squandered. If only he could get everything back... However, he is unable to do so.

When it comes to retirement, don't be afraid to take the plunge. Accept it. You've worked hard your whole life to reach where you are now, and now you have the opportunity to invest in the world's most valuable commodity: time.

It's the one purchase you'll never be sorry for.

7) Have a Goal in Mind!

Earning money has been a major goal of yours for the majority of your life. Make sure you have a new reason to get out of bed every day once you retire.

It will also be easier to spend your money if you adopt or acknowledge a new type of retirement purpose.

You're looking for a reason to do something, not a reason not to.

www.ingramcontent.com/pod-product-compliance
Lightning Source LLC
Chambersburg PA
CBHW071312130726
47997CB00007B/2522